CLASSIC *f*M

GW00470023

HALL *of* FAME

Piano Collection

Highlights from the ultimate classical chart

FABER *ff* MUSIC

Faber Music in association with Classic FM, a Global Radio station.
Faber Music is the exclusive print publisher for all Global Radio sheet music product.

© 2011 Faber Music Ltd
First published in 2011 by Faber Music Ltd
Bloomsbury House 74–77 Great Russell Street London WC1B 3DA
Music processed by Jeanne Roberts
Cover design by Sue Clarke
Cover photograph © istockphoto.com/Alberto Fuentes
Printed in England by Caligraving Ltd
All rights reserved

ISBN10: 0-571-53612-3
EAN13: 978-0-571-53612-2

To buy Faber Music/Global Radio publications, or to find out about the full range of titles available,
please contact your local retailer, or go to www.fabermusic.com or www.classicfm.com/shop.
For sales enquiries, contact Faber Music at sales@fabermusic.com or tel: +44(0)1279 828982.

Contents

Clarinet Concerto

Slow movement theme

At number 2 in the chart, this beautiful work was written in the last few months of Mozart's life. He completed it in just over a week.

Wolfgang Amadeus Mozart

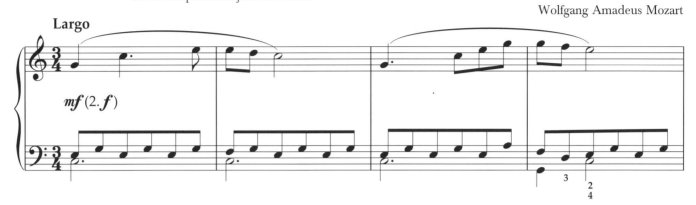

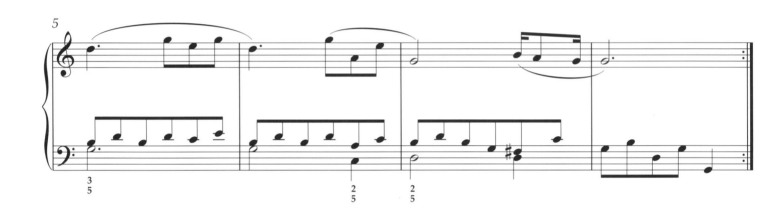

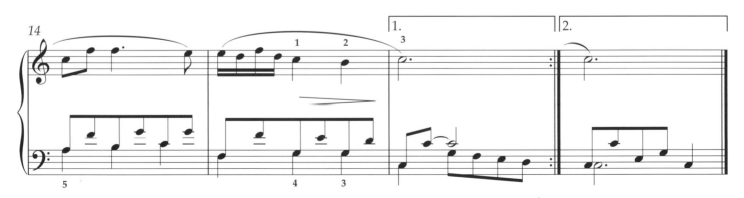

© 2011 by Faber Music Ltd

Symphony No.6 (Pastoral)

First movement theme

Appearing at number 7 in the chart, this is one of Beethoven's few programmatic works,
which is in five rather than the usual four movements.

Ludwig van Beethoven

© 2011 by Faber Music Ltd

Enigma Variations

Nimrod

Elgar depicts his friends through this theme and 14 variations, appearing at number 8 in
the chart.

Edward Elgar

© 2010 by Faber Music Ltd

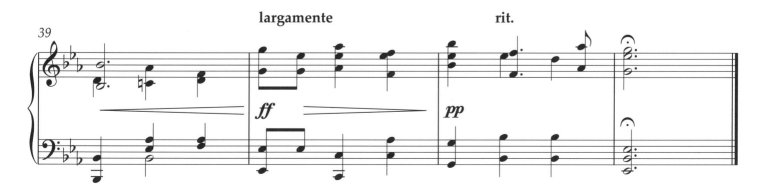

Symphony No.9

Ode to Joy

Beethoven's 9th symphony appears at number 9 in the chart! This is the famous last
movement: Beethoven's setting of Schiller's 'Ode to Joy'.

Ludwig van Beethoven

Allegro assai

© 2011 by Faber Music Ltd

Canon

Pachelbel's most famous piece was originally scored for three violins and basso continuo.
It appears at number 10 of the chart.

Johann Pachelbel

© 2010 by Faber Music Ltd

Fantasia on a Theme by Thomas Tallis

This popular piece brought Vaughan Williams his first major public success at its premiere in 1910. It is number 14 in the ultimate chart.

Ralph Vaughan Williams

© 2008 by The Vaughan Williams Charitable Trust
This arrangement © 2011 by The Vaughan Williams Charitable Trust

The Pearl Fishers' Duet

Au fond du temple saint

At number 15 is Bizet's opera *The Pearl Fishers*, his most successful opera after *Carmen*,
best-known for its great friendship duet, *Au fond du temple saint*.

Georges Bizet

© 2010 by Faber Music Ltd

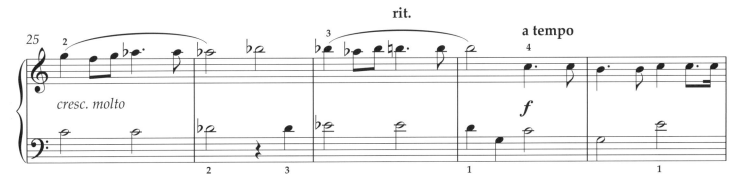

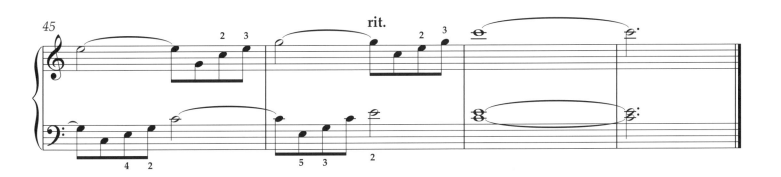

Requiem Mass

Lacrimosa

Much controversy surrounds Mozart's *Requiem* as he died before completing it. It appears
at number 19 of the ultimate chart.

Wolfgang Amadeus Mozart

© 2011 by Faber Music Ltd

The Four Seasons

Slow movement theme from Winter

This set of four violin concertos, one for each season, appears at number 21 of the chart.

Antonio Vivaldi

© 2011 by Faber Music Ltd

The 'Trout' Piano Quintet

Fourth movement theme

Taking its name from the fourth movement theme (based on Schubert's Lied 'Die Forelle'),
the Trout Quintet is number 65 in the chart.

Franz Schubert

© 2011 by Faber Music Ltd

Miserere

At number 23 in the chart is Allegri's *Miserere*: a setting of Psalm 51 for two choirs, generally agreed to be one of the finest examples of polyphony of the Renaissance period.

Gregorio Allegri

© 2007 by Faber Music Ltd

Requiem Mass

Pie Jesu

This is the most famous movement of Fauré's seven-movement funeral mass, which was
written over three years between 1887 and 1890. It appears at number 25 of the chart.

Gabriel Fauré

© 2010 by Faber Music Ltd

1812 Overture

At number 34 in the chart is Tchaikovsky's *1812 Overture*, commissioned to commemorate
Napoleon's defeat in Russia in 1812. Tchaikovsky himself described it as 'very loud
and noisy'!

Piotr Ilyich Tchaikovsky

© 2011 by Faber Music Ltd

Scheherazade

The Young Prince and the Young Princess

At number 35, Rimsky-Korsakov's most celebrated composition is a setting of episodes from *The Arabian Nights*.

Nicolai Rimsky-Korsakov

© 2010 by Faber Music Ltd

Romance

from *The Gadfly*

At number 45 is Shostakovich's 'Romance' from his 1955 film score of *The Gadfly*.

Dmitri Shostakovich

© Copyright by Boosey and Hawkes Music Publishers Ltd.
For the UK, British Commonwealth (ex. Canada) and Eire
This arrangement © Copyright 2011 by Boosey and Hawkes Music Publishers Ltd. Reproduced by permission.

Rhapsody in Blue

At number 46 in the chart, Gershwin's *Rhapsody in Blue* brought together the classical and
jazz worlds and was an immediate success.

George Gershwin

Slowly, with expression

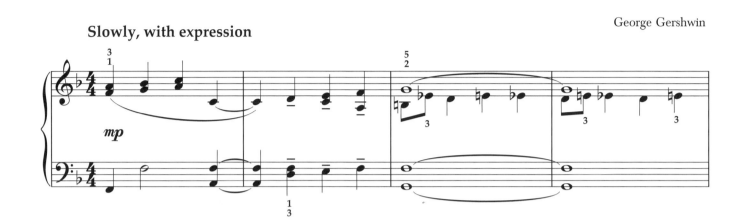

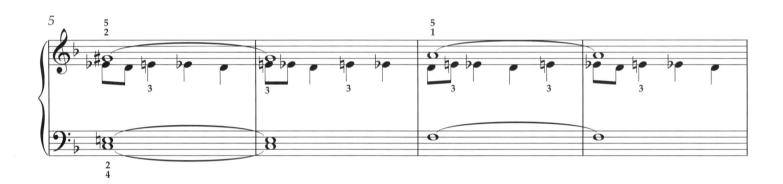

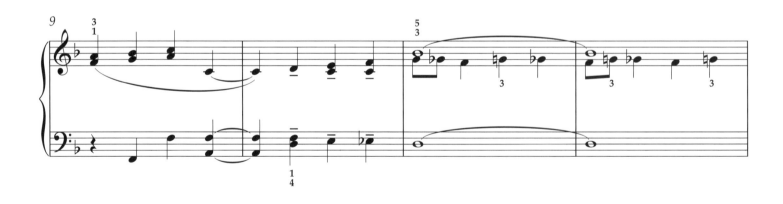

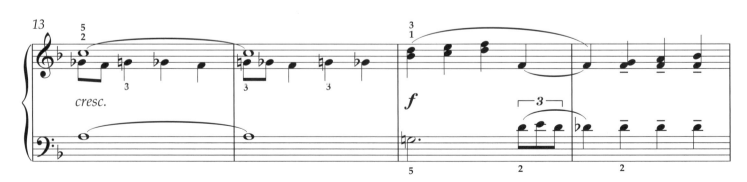

© 2009 by Faber Music Ltd

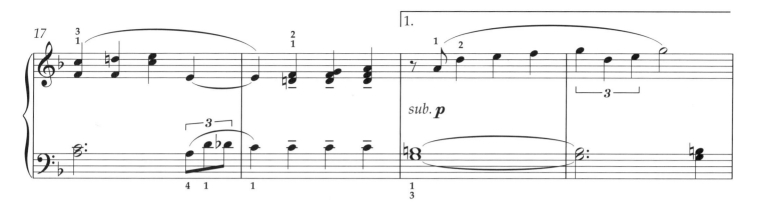
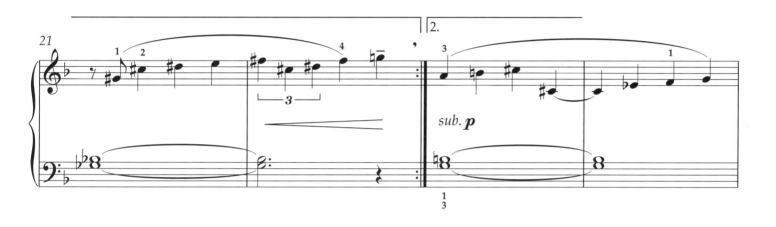
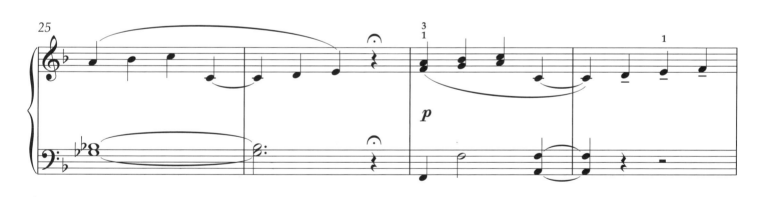
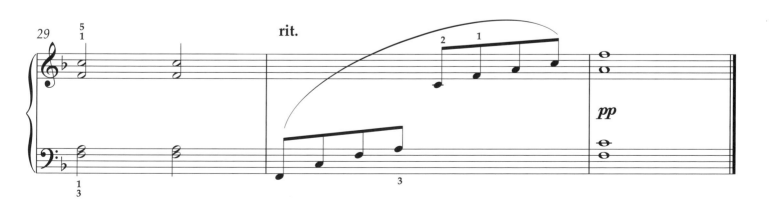

ALSO AVAILABLE
FROM FABER MUSIC AND
CLASSIC *f*M

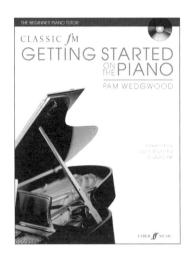

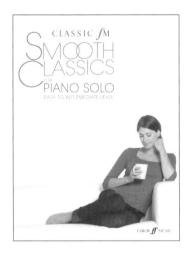

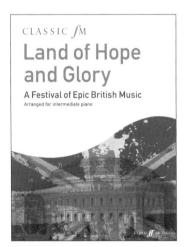

Chopin Piano Favourites	0-571-53461-9	Play the Classics	0-571-53610-7
Christmas Favourites	0-571-53480-5	Relaxation	0-571-53613-1
Classics for Children	0-571-53578-X	Romantic Classics	0-571-53481-3
Getting Started on the Piano	0-571-53477-5	Silent Nights	0-571-53569-0
Hall of Fame	0-571-536123	Smooth Classics	0-571-53478-3
Land of Hope and Glory	0-571-53479-1	The Wedding Collection	0-571-53614-X

FABER *ff* MUSIC

To buy Faber Music publications or to find out about the full range of titles available
please contact your local music retailer or Faber Music sales enquiries:

Faber Music Ltd, Burnt Mill, Elizabeth Way, Harlow CM20 2HX
Tel: +44 (0) 1279 82 89 82   Fax: +44 (0) 1279 82 89 83
sales@fabermusic.com   fabermusic.com   expressprintmusic.com